P9-DNV-910

GOD'S TIMING
*Y*our For *L*ife

DUTCH SHEETS

Regal

From Gospel Light
Ventura, California, U.S.A.

PUBLISHED BY REGAL BOOKS
FROM GOSPEL LIGHT
VENTURA, CALIFORNIA, U.S.A.
PRINTED IN THE U.S.A.

Regal

Regal Books is a ministry of Gospel Light, a Christian publisher dedicated to serving the local church. We believe God's vision for Gospel Light is to provide church leaders with biblical, user-friendly materials that will help them evangelize, disciple and minister to children, youth and families.

It is our prayer that this Regal book will help you discover biblical truth for your own life and help you meet the needs of others. May God richly bless you.

For a free catalog of resources from Regal Books/Gospel Light, please call your Christian supplier or contact us at 1-800-4-GOSPEL or www.regalbooks.com.

All Scripture quotations, unless otherwise indicated, are taken from the *New American Standard Bible* © 1960, 1962, 1963, 1968, 1971, 1972, 1973, 1975, 1977 by The Lockman Foundation. Used by permission.

Other versions used are:
NIV—Scripture taken from the *Holy Bible, New International Version®*. Copyright © 1973, 1978, 1984 by International Bible Society. Used by permission of Zondervan Publishing House. All rights reserved.
KJV—New King James Version. Authorized King James Version.

© Copyright 2001 Dutch Sheets
All rights reserved.

Cover and Interior Design by Robert Williams
Edited by Wil Simon

Library of Congress Cataloging-in-Publication Data
Sheets, Dutch.
        God's timing for your life/Dutch Sheets.
              p. cm.
        Includes bibliographical references.
        ISBN 0-8307-2763-9 (pbk.)
Christian life. 2. Time—Religious aspects—Christianity. I. Title.

BV4509.5 S45 2001
243—dc21   00-068786

Rights for publishing this book outside the U.S.A. or in non-English languages are adminis-tered by Gospel Light Worldwide, an international not-for-profit ministry. For additional information, please visit www.glww.org, email info@glww.org, or write to Gospel Light Worldwide, 1957 Eastman Avenue, Ventura, CA 93003, U.S.A.

Contents

Chapter One 5
The Divine Shift

Chapter Two 15
The Joining of the Seasons

Chapter Three 26
The Fullness of Time

Chapter Four 38
Baca Boot Camp

Chapter Five 48
Keys to Unlocking the Shift

Bibliography 63

Endnotes 64

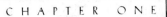

The Divine Shift

The story is told of a man who rushed into a suburban railroad station one morning and, almost breathlessly, asked the ticket agent: "When does the 8:01 train leave?"

"At 8:01," was the answer.

"Well," the man replied, "it is 7:59 by my watch, 7:57 by the town clock, and 8:04 by the station clock. Which time am I to go by?"

"You can go by any clock you wish," said the agent, "but you cannot go by the 8:01 train, for it has already left."

God's time is moving forward hour by hour, minute by minute. There are multitudes who seem to think they can live by any schedule they choose and that, in their own time, they can turn to God. But His time is the right time.[1]

Jesus wept over Jerusalem, saying, "You did not recognize the time of your visitation" (Luke 19:44). They missed the train.

A group of Israelites decided to try and possess the land of Canaan the day after God told them the opportunity had passed. They were routed by the Canaanites (see Num. 14:39-45). The train had already departed.

Ecclesiastes tells us that God is a God of timing: "There is an appointed time for everything. And there is a time for every event under heaven" (Eccles. 3:1).

We need to understand the timings and seasons God ordains for our lives, ministries, cities and nations. Too often we try to reap during planting season, plant during harvest, run when we should be resting and rest when it is time to run. Doing even the right thing at the wrong time, well intentioned as it may be, will cause us to miss the train every time.

Discerning the Times

One of the tribes of Israel, the sons of Issachar, had an ability to discern timing: "men who understood the times, with knowledge of what Israel should do" (1 Chron. 12:32). Notice that it was their ability to understand the times that gave them insight as to what to do. Understanding God's timing is often one of the keys to taking the proper action.

Several months ago, while ministering in Washington, D.C., I was meditating on Daniel 2:20,21:

Let the name of God be blessed forever and ever, for wisdom and power belong to Him. And it is He who changes the times and the epochs [seasons]; He removes kings and establishes kings; He gives wisdom to wise men, and knowledge to men of understanding.

As I reflected on these verses, the Holy Spirit clearly spoke to my heart, *I am shifting things in the Spirit over this city.* I realized immediately that the prayers of God's people were making a difference. We were moving into an opportunity for great advances, perhaps even revival in America. I spoke that morning on "The Divine Shift" and have shared the message several times since.

I want you to understand and recognize the divine shifts in your life—moments when God changes the times and seasons. That is the purpose of this book. Never again do I want you to be sitting in the train station with your bags packed and ticket in hand, watching the train that was to carry you into God's purpose for your life disappearing into the distance.

One of the great disasters of history took place in 1271. Nicolo and Matteo Polo (the father and uncle of Marco) were visiting the Kublai Khan, at that time a world ruler over China, India and all of the East. He was attracted to the story of Christianity as Nicolo and Matteo told it to him and said this to them: "You shall go to your high priest and tell him on my behalf to send me 100 men skilled in your religion, and I shall be baptized. And when I am baptized, all my barons and great men will be baptized and their subjects will receive baptism, too. So there will be more Christians here than there are in your parts." However, nothing was done for about 30 years. Then two or three missionaries were sent—too few and too late. It baffles the imagination to think what a difference to the world it would have made if China had become fully Christian in the thirteenth century and the East had been given to Christ. These men missed the opportunity, and God's purpose was frustrated.[2]

Could it be that God was trying to create an incredible shift that would have changed the course of history? We may never know, but it certainly sounds possible. It is my belief and desire that nothing like that will happen in our generation. When God wants to change the times and seasons or change the heart of a king, I want it to occur.

The following three verses in Isaiah speak of God's change into new seasons:

You have heard; look at all this. And you, will you not declare it? I proclaim to you new things from this time, even hidden things which you have not known (Isa. 48:6).

Behold, I will do something new, now it will spring forth; will you not be aware of it? I will even make a roadway in the wilderness, rivers in the desert (Isa. 43:19).

Behold, the former things have come to pass, now I declare new things; before they spring forth I proclaim them to you (Isa. 42:9).

First, notice the phrase "spring forth" in the last two verses. These words mark a shift in time. Something new is about to spring forth. "Will you not be aware of it?" He asks. Often, God waits until the last moment to move. But it is also true that when He does move, it can transpire quickly. Never give up. Your shift may be closer than you think.

Shortly after Dallas Seminary was founded in 1924, it almost folded. It came to the point of bankruptcy. All the creditors were ready to foreclose at 12:00 noon on a particular day. That morning, the founders of the school met in the president's office to pray that God would provide. In that prayer meeting was Harry Ironside. When it was his turn to pray, he said in his refreshingly candid way, "Lord, we know that the cattle on a thousand hills are Thine. Please sell some of them and send us the money."

Just about that time, a tall Texan wearing boots and an open-collar shirt strolled into the business office. "Howdy!" he said to the secretary. "I just sold two carloads of cattle over in Fort Worth. I've been trying to make a business deal go through, but it just won't work. I feel God wants me to give this money to the seminary. I don't know if you need it or not, but here's the check," and he handed it over.

The secretary took the check and, knowing something of the critical nature of the hour, went to the door of the prayer meeting and timidly tapped. Dr. Lewis Sperry Chafer, the founder and president of the school, answered the door and took the check from her hand. When he looked at the amount, it was for the exact sum of the debt. Then he recognized the name on the check as that of the cattleman. Turning to Dr. Ironside, he said, "Harry, God sold the cattle."[3]

Second, notice the word "new." Again, this word speaks of a shift. In the New Testament, two Greek words are translated "new," although they have different meanings. Understanding the difference is important.

The word *neos* means numerically new but not different. For instance, if you buy a brand-new car of a certain make and model, you have a new car, but there are hundreds more just like it all over the country. It's new but it's not different. It's the same as others—it's just new. The other Greek word for "new" is *kainos*, which means not only numerically new but also qualitatively new. This refers, for example, to a car manufactured today as compared to a Model T car. Not only is this a numerically new car, but it is also qualitatively new because it's different.

Distinguishing the difference between these two words—*neos* and *kainos*—is very important to our proper understanding of Scripture. Second Corinthians 5:17 says that we are new (*kainos*) creations. We're not just duplications, or replicas, of something else, which would be *neos*. We're new in the sense of being different—*kainos*. We're qualitatively new. We are new creations—brand-new in kind and quality. God has put a different nature in us, transformed us and put the power of His Spirit in us. When we're born again, we're not just the same people with a few changes; we are *kainos*—brand-new on the inside.

In Matthew 9:17, Jesus used both of these Greek words in one statement when He referred to the practice of putting new wine into new wineskins. He said that new (*neos*) wine needed to be put into new (*kainos*) wineskins. This new wine of the Spirit is not something different but, rather, more of the same. The Holy Spirit can't change and He cannot improve, so it isn't qualitatively new wine. He desires to put more of Himself into us—numerically new wine.

Although the wine isn't different, the wineskin does need to change. We, the wineskins, need to be *kainos*, or qualitatively new. In order to get another dose of His Spirit poured into us, we must be transformed and changed from one stage to another. If we don't become different—qualitatively new—we won't be able to hold the new wine He is pouring out. We will miss this new "time." To prevent this, He puts us through processes of change. If we let Him work in our lives to transform us, then He can put more of

God is continually preparing us for more wine, for another dose of pouring out His Spirit. These changes may not always be fun, but they are always good.

Himself, His Spirit, into us. He can put new (*neos*) wine into new (*kainos*) wineskins.

Thus, in order for God to prepare us for the new season, He changes us. He has done an enormous amount of change in me the past couple of years. When it comes to His work in us, I've realized that God doesn't have the phrase "That's good enough" in His vocabulary. He is continually preparing us for more wine, for another dose of pouring out His Spirit. These changes may not always be fun, but they are always good.

From time to time, lobsters have to leave their shells in order to grow. They need the shell to protect them from being torn apart; yet when they grow, the old shell must be abandoned. If they did not abandon it, the old shell would soon become their prison and finally their casket.

The tricky part for the lobster is the brief period of time between when the old shell is discarded and the new one is formed. During that terribly vulnerable period, the transition must be scary to the lobster. Ocean currents gleefully cartwheel them from coral to kelp. Hungry schools of fish are ready to make them a part of their food chain. For a while at least, that old shell must look pretty good.

We are not so different from lobsters. To change and grow, we must sometimes shed our shells—a structure, a framework—that we've depended on. Discipleship means being so committed to Christ that when He bids us to follow, we will change, risk, grow and leave our "shells" behind.[4]

Like the lobster, I like the new shell; I just don't like the process.

These two Greek words for "new" are also used for the word "renewal." By adding the prefix "ana," which is equivalent to the English prefix *"re-"*, to the words, we have the two different concepts of renewal. *Ananeoo* is numerically renewed. This is when

God brings back to us something we had before. It isn't qualitatively new, but there is renewal or refreshing. Perhaps He restores to us our first love, or He restores us to a state of faith in which we previously walked.

The other word is *anakainoo,* which means qualitatively renewed. In this type of renewal, God brings another stage of newness, and we are different from anything we've ever been before. This process not only restores us, but it also transforms us into the image of Christ. Rather than just renewing us to where we were, He renews us to a fresh new place. When He is finished, we don't feel or look the same. We are, indeed, different and ready for a shift to more wine.

As another example, the word used for the renewing of the mind, written in Romans 12:2, is *anakainosis,* which means a qualitatively new mind. God wants to renew our minds in the sense that He radically transforms the way we think so that we can participate in the changes He brings and the new thing He does. Shifting with God requires *kainos.*

God is doing new things in the earth, both in the sense of *neos* and *kainos.* He's giving us more of what we've had in the past, but He's also making some radical changes. Unfortunately, some people won't be able to receive these changes because their wineskins aren't *kainos.* They won't be ready to move with God in His process of bringing us from the old to the new. The shift is coming, but will we recognize the timing and will our wineskins be ready?

Finally, notice the word "hidden" in Isaiah 48:6. Have you ever noticed that when God begins to do something new, it is often something that was hidden? He often keeps it a secret right up to the last minute.

Like any loving parent, God likes to surprise us. He has certainly been surprising me lately. A few months ago, as I was praying about some difficult situations, the Lord clearly spoke to me, saying, "It isn't quite time, but very soon I have some surprises for you."

Of course, I'm just like a kid at Christmas. I want to open those packages now! So I started prying. "Well, that's great, God. What are they?"

"I'm not ready to reveal them to you yet. But when the time is right, I have some surprises for you."

Again I tried to find out what He was talking about. "Oh, that's great. Maybe You could just tell me one of them?"

I couldn't get Him to say anything to me except, "I have some surprises for you."

Once the time was right, however, He began the shift, unfolding and revealing the surprises to me. Talk about *new* things *springing forth*! Talk about divine shifts! These *hidden* things—surprises—began to unfold with supernatural speed and sovereign power. Though I do not yet feel released to discuss them, they are wonderful, heavenly surprises.

He has some for you as well. He is changing the times and seasons. Be alert and flexible. Make sure your wineskin is new, ready for the new wine He is about to pour out. Get ready to shift!

When Michigan played Wisconsin in basketball early in the season in 1989, Michigan's Rumeal Robinson stepped to the foul line for two shots late in the fourth quarter. His team trailed by one point, so Rumeal had a good chance of regaining the lead for Michigan. He missed both shots, however, allowing Wisconsin to upset favored Michigan.

Rumeal felt awful about costing his team the game and realized he needed to be better prepared. After each practice for the rest of the season, Rumeal shot 100 extra foul shots.

Thus, Rumeal was ready when he stepped to the foul line to shoot two shots with three seconds left in overtime in the national championship game. Swish went the first shot, and swish went the second. Those shots won Michigan the national championship.[5]

RENEWING THE MIND

1. Have you ever done the right thing at the wrong time? What does Proverbs have to say about choosing the right time to do things?

2. What is the difference between *neos* and *kainos*? How does being *kainos* affect your life?

3. What do you need to shed in your life? Pride? Fear? Religiosity?

The Joining of the Seasons

Julia Dixon had just accidentally locked herself out of her house when the mailman came up the drive.

"Mrs. Dixon!" he exclaimed in concern. "You look upset. What's the matter?"

"Oh, I don't know what I'm going to do," she wailed, wringing her hands nervously. "The door locked behind me, and my neighbor, who keeps a duplicate key for me, is out of town. My husband has a key, but he's at an all-day conference at a hotel downtown, and I doubt I can reach him. How am I going to get back in?"

The mailman tried to calm the woman and advised her to call a locksmith. "I guess that's my only recourse," she agreed, "but to tell you the truth, they charge an arm and a leg and I really can't afford an extra expense right now. Things have been tight."

The mailman commiserated with her but pointed out that she had no choice. "Look, I'd better be on my way," he said, "but here's your mail. Who knows? Maybe there'll be some good news inside one of the letters to cheer you up!"

Julia looked through the envelopes. There was one from her brother Jonathan. He had visited the family the previous week and had stayed for a few days. "I wonder why he's writing so soon," she murmured. When she tore open the letter, a key fell into her palm.

"Dear Julia," the letter began. "Last week, when I was staying at your house and you were out shopping, I accidentally locked myself out. I asked your neighbor for your duplicate but forgot to return it. So I'm enclosing it now."[1]

Now that's good timing! God would probably have made me either wait or break a window. He seems to enjoy testing my patience. Not that I'm complaining—I would never stoop to such carnality.

What Time Do You Keep?

While recently meditating on the divine shift, I thought about the different New Testament words for time, *chronos* and *kairos*. (The word *chronos* refers to the general process of time or chronological time. The word *kairos* refers to the right time, the opportune or strategic time, the now time.) As I was doing this, God began to reveal a very important truth to me. I have always completely separated these two concepts— chronological time and the right time—but God has been showing me that this is not accurate. Often, they are simply different phases of the same process. *Kairos*, in many ways, is an extension or continuation of *chronos*. As the processes of God's plans unfold, *chronos* becomes *kairos*. The new is connected to the old and, in fact, is often the result of what happened in the old. *Kairos*, the opportune time, is literally born of *chronos*, the general time.

When we're in a nonstrategic general season of life's daily routine, plodding along in the *chronos* time, God doesn't totally start over with a *kairos* season. His overall agenda does not change. He simply takes us through one phase of a process in which our perseverance and faithfulness have allowed Him to shift us into the next phase—a strategic season. He changes the time and season, transforming *chronos* into *kairos*.

This should be a great encouragement to you. Perhaps you're in a *chronos* time where you don't feel like anything exciting is happening. This season of your life may even be tedious—a time of plowing, standing, believing and persistent praying. You must understand that all of that is part of a bigger picture. The *chronos* season, however frustrating, is not unimportant. If you press on, doing what is necessary in these general times, the process will shift into a *kairos* season of reaping. Galatians 6:9 says, "Let us not lose heart in doing good, for in due time [*kairos*] we shall reap if we do not grow weary."

When complimented on her homemade biscuits, the cook at a popular Christian conference center told Dr. Harry Ironside, "Just consider what goes into the making of these biscuits. The flour itself doesn't taste good, neither does the baking powder nor the shortening nor the other ingredients. However, when I mix them all together and put them in the oven, they come out just right."

Much of life in the *chronos* season seems tasteless, even bad, but God is able to combine these ingredients of our lives in such a way that a shift occurs and a banquet results.[2]

Life is a series of changes—a process of going from the old to the new—from *chronos* to *kairos*. Growth, change, revival—all are processes. Life is connected. Not understanding this, we tend to despise the *chronos* times of preparing, sowing, believing and persevering. Our preference is to always live in the *kairos* times of fresh and strategic opportunities.

It is important to realize, however, that our actions and attitudes in the *chronos* times are what determine whether or not God can shift us into the *kairos* times. It is in the *chronos* times that the necessary ingredients are added. The old and the new are inseparably linked—different but related. The new doesn't come *in spite* of the old; it comes *because of* what we did during the old. Understanding this will enable us to not grow weary or lose heart in doing good during the *chronos* times.

Our actions and attitudes in the chronos times of preparing, sowing, believing and persevering are what determine whether God can shift us into the kairos times of fresh and strategic opportunities.

Often, as we continue working through difficult times, a mind-set comes to us that life will always be this way. We begin to believe that the *kairos* time is never going to come. If we're not careful, we lose our expectation and our faith begins to waver. We've prayed so long, plowed so long, believed so long and held on for so long that we begin to live with a "so long" mentality. Disillusionment then sets in and our faith is gone.

God wants to shift our thinking from becoming discouraged during these times to realizing the necessity of *chronos* seasons. We're not losing or wasting time, we're investing it. And if we do so faithfully, the shift *will* come. Knowing that we are cooperating with God and giving Him what He needs to bring the new, we can rejoice over, rather than despise, small beginnings. We won't despair about prayer meetings that go on for several years with little apparent fruit. Our faith is based only on the truth of God's Word and obedience to it.

The Time to Plant and Grow

Jean Giono tells the story of Elzeard Bouffier, a shepherd he met in 1913 in the French Alps.

At that time, because of careless deforestation, the mountains around Provence, France, were barren. Former villages were deserted because their springs and brooks had run dry. The wind blew furiously, unimpeded by foliage.

While mountain climbing, Giono came to a shepherd's hut, where he was invited to spend the night.

After dinner, Giono watched the shepherd meticulously sort through a pile of acorns, discarding those that were cracked or undersized. When the shepherd had counted out 100 perfect acorns, he stopped for the night and went to bed.

Giono learned that the 55-year-old shepherd had been planting trees on the wild hillsides for over three years. He had planted 100,000 trees, 20,000 of which had sprouted. Of those, he expected half to be eaten by rodents or die due to the elements, and the other half to live.

After World War I, Giono returned to the mountainside and discovered an incredible rehabilitation: there was a veritable forest, accompanied by a chain reaction in nature. Water flowed in the once-empty brooks. The ecology, sheltered by a leafy roof and bonded to the earth by a mat of spreading roots, became hospitable. Willows, rushes, meadows, gardens and flowers were birthed.

Giono returned again after World War II. Twenty miles from the lines, the shepherd had continued his work, ignoring the war of 1939, just as he had ignored that of 1914. The reformation of the land continued. Whole regions glowed with health and prosperity.

Giono wrote:

> On the site of the ruins I had seen in 1913 now stand neat farms. . . . The old streams, fed by the rains and snows that the forest conserves, are flowing again, . . . Little by little, the villages have been rebuilt. People from the plains, where land is costly, have settled here, bringing youth, motion, the spirit of adventure.[3]

When we persevere during the *chronos* seasons, we are like spiritual reforesters, digging holes in barren land and planting the seeds of life. Through these seeds, dry spiritual wastelands are transformed into harvestable fields, and life-giving water is brought to parched and barren places.[4]

When we are properly prepared and the time is right, God can shift seasons very quickly. Overnight, it seems, He transforms dry times into rivers, barrenness into fruitfulness and makes a way where there is no way. Timing is a factor; but when it's right, God causes the shift, and the *chronos* changes into *kairos*. Allow this truth to bring faith and encouragement into your situation.

Let's look at some biblical examples to help us see this concept more clearly.

Abraham received a glorious promise from God that he would have a son through Sarah and that his descendants would be in number as the stars in the sky. He then moved into a

24-year *chronos* season of having to persevere and walk by faith. After this, as recorded in Genesis 18:10, God appeared to him and said, in essence, that a divine shift was about to happen: "I will surely return to you at this time next year; and behold, Sarah your wife shall have a son." (The word for "time" is *eth*, the Hebrew counterpart for the Greek word *kairos*—strategic, or opportune, time.)

After so many years in the *chronos* season, Abraham and Sarah laughed at this prospect. Abraham even tried to get God to fulfill His plans through Ishmael. But true to His word, God created the shift; He changed the times and the seasons. Because Abraham had walked with Him—even though he didn't do it perfectly—through this long and sometimes tedious season, God changed it to a strategic, opportune time. Abraham and Sarah moved from *chronos* to *kairos*. The new sprang forth from the old, and Isaac, the son of promise, was born.

Another example can be seen in the process the Israelites went through in their journey to the Promised Land. Israel was in a difficult *chronos* season of having to persevere and wait in Egypt. Suddenly, the shift sprang forth. When the time was right, God, in His great wisdom and power, moved quickly and said, in effect, "I am changing the season."

As a part of the process, God came to Moses, who had ended up on the backside of a desert for his own 40-year *chronos* season, and told him He was about to shift things through him. Moses essentially said, "Shift them with somebody else, not me." But God made it clear to Moses that he was the one to deliver the Israelites out of Egypt, and God brought about the divine shift for Moses and for the nation of Israel.

In a sad turn of events, these Israelites weren't able to lay hold, by faith, of this *kairos* season, and they lost it. They ended up in another *chronos* season, wandering in the wilderness for 40 years. The next generation, who would eventually go in and possess the land, also had to wait through this difficult *chronos* period. Suddenly, God came to Joshua and said that in three days they were to go across into the Promised Land. God was creating the divine shift. The wandering time was over, and He moved the nation into a new phase. He quickly brought them from *chronos* into *kairos*.

If we have been in a long *chronos* season, our tendency is to think that it's not possible to shift quickly into a *kairos* time. But it is imperative for us to be prepared to change when God says He's bringing the shift. We have to move with Him, or we will miss what He wants to do. If we don't understand the ways of God, we can become so confused and frustrated that we aren't able to reach out in faith and change. Like the first generation of Israelites that came out of Egypt, we end up in the wilderness and never reach the promise. However, if we comprehend the ways of God, this will decrease the frustration during the waiting time. We can move into peace and rest, knowing that God is in control and we are walking with Him.

Saul, who later became the apostle Paul, received a divine visitation from God on the road to Damascus. When the Lord revealed Himself to Saul, he experienced a dramatic conversion—a *kairos* time. He then shifted into a routine *chronos* season where, for 12 to 13 years, God was transforming him and bringing great revelation. When the time was right, as recorded in Acts 13, the Lord declared that Paul was to be separated for the work to which he was called. This *chronos* time became *kairos* time as God released Paul into the fullness of his ministry. The routine time wasn't wasted. It was all a part of the process of training and preparation for what God was going to launch him into. *Chronos* shifted into *kairos,* and the world has never been the same since.

The Strategic Location

Captain Ralph and his only crew member, Shaun, had dropped off their passengers at the Northwest town of Poulsbo and were on their regular route back to Seattle. A fierce storm had developed and, as they reentered Puget Sound on the luxury yacht *The Matchmaker,* they heard an urgent radio transmission.

Strong winds had tipped over a sailboat, sending a man and woman into the frigid waters of Puget Sound. The man had made it to shore, but the woman was missing. A helicopter and rescue boats were crisscrossing the area where the woman had fallen into the water; but after almost two hours they were beginning to lose hope of finding her. It was doubtful she could still be alive after that much time in the icy cold water.

The Matchmaker was quite a ways from the rescue operation, but Captain Ralph realized their location was strategic. Having traversed the sound many times, he was very familiar with its currents. He told Shaun that the woman would no longer be in the area of the capsized boat, but by now would have been carried by the strong current directly into their path. Because of the storm, it was impossible for any other boat to get to that area in time to try and save her.

Recognizing they were this woman's only opportunity for rescue, Captain Ralph and Shaun strained to see or hear anything that might help them find her in the midst of the storm. Suddenly they heard a faint noise that sounded like a bird. As Captain Ralph turned the boat so the lights of Seattle could illuminate the water, they saw the woman crying out to them for help. While Captain Ralph maneuvered the boat into position, Shaun pulled the desperate woman aboard. Collapsing at Shaun's feet, she grasped his legs while thanking him again and again. Imagine her relief upon seeing *The Matchmaker's* approach! She had been watching the rescue operation disappear farther and farther into the distance as the current swept her away.

A routine journey became a strategic event, and a woman's life was saved. Be ready. Like Captain Ralph, you may be the one God has prepared for a specific *kairos*.

I remember when God caused the Iron Curtain in Europe to be destroyed in the early 1990s. People had prayed for decades to break down the oppression of Communist regimes that held millions of people in bondage. It didn't look like this would ever happen. But suddenly God changed the times and the seasons. He created the divine shift, and the face of Europe was rapidly changed in just a very short amount of time—different governments, different leaders, different names of nations. God had the necessary wisdom and power to bring the divine shift very quickly.

He can do the same for us. Persevere in the *chronos*—the routine. *Kairos* is coming!

RENEWING THE MIND

1. What event in your life has required years of patience and long-suffering? Have you seen any fruit from laboring faithfully over the years?

2. Is it possible that God wants us to be faithful in believing for certain events to happen, even though we may not see

them become reality or come to completion in our lifetime? Does the Bible offer examples of this?

3. Do you view the *chronos* and *kairos* seasons of your life as being independent of each other or connected?

4. What are some of the effects of not waiting on God's timing for something to happen?

5. What gives you strength to wait upon the Lord's timing when it comes to issues in your life and relationships with people?

The Fullness of Time

When God shifts us from a general *chronos* time to an opportune *kairos* time, it doesn't mean that the process and the fight of faith are finished. It means we have shifted into a very strategic season where the opportunity is great, but we're not yet to full fruitfulness. There is still a persevering that needs to happen.

The Bible speaks not only of *chronos* and *kairos*, but also of a *pleroo*, or fullness of time. Galatians 4:4 reads, "But when the fulness of the time came, God sent forth His Son, born of a woman, born under the Law."

This word "fullness" indicates fully completing or finishing something. Whereas *kairos* indicates opportunity to perform a task or produce fruit, *pleroo* means it has been accomplished.

This could be likened to the process of bringing forth children. After conception, a woman goes through all three stages of timing: *chronos, kairos* and *pleroma*. For nine months, she faithfully endures the challenging but important developmental stage of *chronos*. Much is happening in the hidden place of the womb, but she cannot yet hold and fully enjoy the fruit she knows is coming.

She then moves into the *kairos* stage of labor and delivery. She hasn't yet come to fullness, but it is near. This *kairos* time is very difficult and dangerous, however. Opportunity doesn't guarantee success. There will be much work, pain and pushing if the fullness stage of birth is to be reached.

There have been very few times in my relationship with my wife when she was totally unreasonable, where intelligent discussion was impossible. In fact, there have been only two times—the births of our daughters, Sarah and Hannah.

These *kairos* times were very precarious for me. I loved my wife and wanted to help but, contrary to her clearly articulated wishes, stopping the process of delivery was impossible. I also loved our babies and wanted the processes to continue, difficult as they were. And last, I loved myself and wanted to continue living. At one point, my life was hanging by a thread. Thankfully, the decision to continue wasn't made by me but by God.

Finally, a woman goes from the *kairos* season into the *pleroma* stage of fullness, and the baby is born. It is always worth the pain of the process when this occurs.

The Nature of Birthing Something New

Spiritual births are also difficult and dangerous. Unlike a woman in labor, however, we can give up during these strategic times and stop the delivery process. It is often a hazardous and precarious time; disillusionment, weariness, confusion and other problems can easily arise.

F. B. Meyer uses the illustration of a beehive to compare the struggle of bees to that of the Christian:

A beekeeper told me the story of a hive—how, when the little bee is in the first stage, it is put into a hexagonal cell, and honey enough is stored there for its use until it reaches maturity. The honey is sealed with a capsule of wax, and when the tiny bee has fed itself on the honey and exhausted the supply, the time has come for it to emerge into the open. But, oh, the wrestle, the tussle, the straining to get through that wax! It is the strait gate for the bee, so strait that in the agony of exit the bee rubs off the membrane that hid its wings, and on the other side it is able to fly!

Once a moth got into the hive, fed on the wax capsules and the bees got out without any strain or trouble. But they could not fly; and the other bees stung them to death.[1]

Are you struggling to get to the next stage? Don't give up. Your struggles won't be wasted; they may even be necessary. The key is not to quit.

Consider the disciples of Christ. They went through three intense years with Jesus. Then came *kairos*—the Cross, the Resurrection, the Ascension and Pentecost. They were very close to their fullness of time. But like many of us, they came extremely close to losing the "baby" in this transition between *kairos* and *pleroo*.

At one crucial point, they were confused because they didn't understand what was happening. God was truly moving behind the scenes, but things were not unfolding the way the disciples had envisioned. In their confusion, they came to a point of frustration where they basically looked at one another and said, "What are we going to do?"

For three years, Jesus had been there; then they watched Him die. He was raised from the dead and they were excited, but He left again and something about it seemed permanent this time. He was gone. He had talked about the Holy Spirit coming, but that didn't make much sense. It would have seemed more logical if Jesus had just stayed.

Peter spoke up first (can you believe that?) and said, "I am going fishing" (John 21:3). He was essentially saying, "I'm going back to what I was doing three years ago. I'm returning to the only thing I know and understand. The dream is over. I don't know where God is going, but I'm going back to my business. I'm going fishing."

He and the others had come through the *chronos* season and had shifted into the *kairos* strategic time. Just before fullness, they came extremely close to losing the "baby." Only a few days later, Pentecost occurred, and we see what they almost lost. Through Peter's first sermon as a born-again believer filled with the Spirit of God, 3,000 people came to Christ. As a group, the disciples then proceeded to turn their world upside down (see Acts 17:6, *KJV*). Fullness had come.

Birth Pains of My Own

I have personally experienced the difficulty of these God-given shifts. I waited seven years through a lot of plowing and difficult times for God to give our church certain breakthroughs. When He started making the change from *chronos* to *kairos*, it wasn't in the way I expected. At times, I must admit it was confusing and disturbing. A part of me knew that it was God orchestrating the shift that was happening, yet it was so different from what I had envisioned that it was challenging for me to process.

Until the plan actually began to unfold, I had absolutely no idea it would happen the way it did. I found myself in places where I had many opportunities to lose heart and waver. I had gone through *chronos* and come to *kairos*, where God said, "I'm beginning to fulfill the vision I gave you." But the events that occurred were totally opposite from what I expected.

My associate pastor came to me and said he would like to plant a church in our city. He was willing to wait or go to another city, but his heart was in Colorado Springs. After much prayer, I believed he was indeed supposed to plant a church in this city.

Making what I believed to be a very selfless decision, I released him to do this. I also encouraged any staff and church members who were feeling led by the Holy Spirit to go with him and help plant this church to do so. We guessed that 10 to 15 percent of the congregation would go.

Satan, however, began to create rumors and scenarios to make it appear that it wasn't a peaceful church plant, but rather a church split. One of the rumors was that this associate was really being forced out so that I could bring in someone else. Though we both tried, we couldn't overcome this lie. Several people believed I was lying to protect myself, and the other brother was graciously covering me in my sin. Offenses were picked up.

The irony was that in perhaps the most unselfish thing I've ever done, I received the greatest slander and criticism. And rather than 15 percent of the congregation going to help him, closer to 40 percent went.

I saw this coming and several times I considered stopping the plant, but the Holy Spirit wouldn't allow me to. He simply instructed me to let it progress and assured me He would take care of us. He spoke to me of the surprises I mentioned in chapter 1.

In this very fragile *kairos* time, I had to be sure not to get sidetracked by current circumstances and get my eyes off the big picture. There were many opportunities to lose heart. I had numerous talks with God, asking, "Is this really You? Have we truly heard You say to do these things? Did You really allow this to happen? Because if You told us to do these things and we're walking in obedience to You, then I know everything will be fine. I'm okay with what outwardly looks totally opposite of what I think it should look like, as long as I know You're in control."

There is a small anecdote that I think encapsulates this difficult time for me:

The only survivor of a shipwreck washed up on a small uninhabited island. He cried out to God to save him, and every day he scanned the horizon for help, but none seemed forthcoming.

Exhausted, he eventually managed to build a rough hut and put his few possessions in it. But then one day, after hunting for food, he arrived home to find his little hut in flames, the smoke rolling up to the sky. The worst had happened; he was stung with grief.

Early the next day, though, a ship drew near the island and rescued him.

"How did you know I was here?" he asked the crew.

"We saw your smoke signal," they replied.

Though it may not seem so now, your present difficulty may be instrumental to your future happiness.[2]

I had to keep reminding myself of God's faithfulness and that if *I* did what He said, *He* would do what He said. Then, true to His word, within just a very short time, God supernaturally moved in ways far beyond what could have happened had we not obeyed Him and made the changes. The "new" and "hidden" things—the surprises—began to "spring forth." We are not yet in fullness, but we have certainly moved into the birthing stage.

Paul said words to the effect, "I glory in my weakness that His strength can be perfected in my weakness" (see 2 Cor. 12:9,10). When the shift into *kairos* comes, there are simply going to be some things that we don't understand. In our humanness, we tend to plan everything out in our minds and envision the scenario of how we believe things will occur. When it doesn't happen that way, another part of our humanness kicks in and begins to question everything. This is a time when we are extremely vulnerable. The inclination to say "I'm going fishing . . . I've had it . . . I'm finished" can be very strong.

Let's apply this understanding of God's timing and the possible pitfalls to praying for revival by the Body of Christ. Who is the most vulnerable to disillusionment? Those who have been the most passionate for revival are the ones most susceptible to frustration and to losing heart. Proverbs 13:12 states, "Hope deferred makes the heart sick." The portion of the Body of Christ that is okay with the way things are and hasn't really been interceding for revival isn't going to become disillusioned with anything. In their minds, everything is fine. As long as the economy is good, most Americans—including Christians—are happy. It's the people who have been crying out to God for years, those who are passionately desirous for revival in the land, who struggle the most with hope deferred and disillusionment.

If you are believing for a miracle in your life, you're a lot more likely to experience hope deferred than the person who doesn't expect anything to happen. Here's the paradox: A person who is more passionate for God is more at risk of spiritual disillusionment than a person who has little or no passion or commitment.

Be Ready When the Divine Shift Comes

At the Pool of Bethesda, Jesus came to the man who had been in his paralyzed condition for 36 years and asked him what seemed to be a strange question: "Do you want to get well?" (John 5:6, *NIV*). The man's answer revealed that although he was waiting at the pool, he really had no hope of being healed. He was in a *kairos* moment, close to *fullness*, but hopelessness had set in.

Jesus asked him this question to make him realize that, although he was waiting for the miraculous stirring in the pool, he had lost all hope of actually being healed. Only seconds away from experiencing the new, just a handclasp away from total restoration, the man was too disillusioned to recognize it. Somewhere along the way, as he went through the processes of time, he lost his expectation. There wasn't anything within him that could respond in hope to Jesus' question.

When God brings a shift, we must be ready to shift with Him. If we're not careful, we won't believe that He can bring us from the *chronos* stages through the *kairos* seasons and into fullness. We must not become so accustomed to working hard and seeing little fruit that, when the time for the shift comes, we don't have the faith to move into the new. God wants to bring the divine shift to our lives, our churches,

We must not become so accustomed to working hard and seeing little fruit that, when the time for the divine shift comes, we don't have the faith to move into the new.

our communities and our nation. When He says it's time to shift, we must take His hand and shift with Him, knowing He can and is willing to do it.

Reader's Digest told of the late Harvey Penick: In the 1920s, Penick bought a red spiral notebook and began jotting down observations about golf. He never showed the book to anyone except his son until 1991, when he shared it with a local writer and asked if he thought it was worth publishing. The man read it and told him yes. He left word with Penick's wife the next evening that Simon & Schuster had agreed to an advance of $90,000.

When the writer saw Penick later, the old man seemed troubled. Finally, Penick came clean. With all his medical bills, he said, there was no way he could advance Simon & Schuster that much money. The writer had to explain that Penick would be the one to receive the $90,000.

His first golf book, *Harvey Penick's Little Red Book*, sold more than a million copies, one of the biggest best-sellers in the history of sports books. His second book, *And If You Play Golf, You're My Friend*, sold nearly three-quarters of a million.[3]

We sometimes live in the routine stage for so long that, like Mr. Penick, we find it difficult to receive the blessing of God when it comes. When He offers the shift, be ready to receive it.

Divine shifts make the devil nervous. He heard all the prophecies about the Messiah, and he held out for eternal *chronos*. Then he saw the Virgin Birth and realized it was *kairos*. He had been dreading it for 4,000 years, couldn't figure out how God was going to do it, then he realized it was unfolding. He saw the shift coming, but when God did it, there was nothing the devil could do to halt the process. He remembers that, and it terrifies him. That's why he works so hard against the Church.

He knows he can't stop God, but maybe he can stop God's people through discouragement, unbelief, apathy or complacency.

We cannot allow this to happen! We must realize that the times of difficulty we walk through are not failures, but seasons of training and preparation. Then, when God says it's time to shift, we must be ready to shift with Him. Yes, He may shake things up, pull us out of our comfort zones and start realigning things. And just like Israel, we may not always like it and may even be comfortable on the backside of the desert. But when God says, "Time to move!" it's decision time very quickly. Will we rearrange what's necessary? Will we adjust our lives so we can go with Him? Or will we miss the shift and what He wants to accomplish?

I believe that in America we are about to shift from plowing to reaping, from the wilderness to Canaan. I think we're about to shift from weakness to strength. God is going to shift people and money. He's going to shift us into a new season of power, signs and wonders, miracles and deliverances. He's going to shift some from sickness to health, from wounds into wholeness, from broken families with prodigals into homes where prodigals now serve God. He is going to use the prayers and plowing we've done in the *chronos* time of the old to create the new things.

God is going to shift things in our schools and move in a powerful way. He's going to break all the man-made rules that try to keep Him out. He's going to show Himself strong on behalf of a generation that doesn't even realize what they want—God. Some will try to stop it, but there won't be anything they can do, because the wind of the Spirit is just going to blow. Revival is going to be in the hallways and the classrooms. Whether the teachers get in on it or not, the youth and children will.

What do you think will happen in some of these schools when someone who has been pushed around in a wheelchair through the halls for years, suddenly is running down the hallway, leaping and praising God, saying, "He healed me!"? This is what occurred in Acts 3, causing great harvest. When God shifts things, testimonies of His powerful workings will resound and many will come to Christ.

We cannot shift the times and the seasons; only God can do that. But we can cooperate with Him; we can be faithful during the *chronos* so that He is able to bring us into the *kairos* and then to fullness. We can persevere and keep ourselves positioned properly. We must guard against lethargy, complacency and unbelief.

We need to anchor ourselves to the truth and stir our faith to believe that God can rapidly orchestrate changes. We must understand the reasons why the *chronos* times are necessary, and we must also remember that God has the ability to shift things very quickly into strategic *kairos* seasons and then to fullness.

We must be prepared and willing to shift with Him. If we are, He will accomplish all that He said He would in and through our lives.

RENEWING THE MIND

1. Have you ever set up your own timetable or perception of how things should happen in your life, but God had a completely different timetable and process? If so, why did you not see God's timing and method? How did this affect how you worked through this situation?

2. Have you experienced the precariousness of the transition from kairos to fullness? What must be remembered during these critical seasons?

3. What effect, if any, does your attitude and preparedness have on the outcome of the various seasons in your life?

Baca Boot Camp

While vacationing in the Smoky Mountains recently, Ceci and I were enjoying the serenity and majesty of a mountain stream. As young, carefree people will sometimes do (yes, I said young!), we began to hop from rock to rock, crossing the stream at various places.

Hand-holding, laughter, pictures flashing—it was exhilarating! Until . . . no, I didn't fall into the stream, but I did fall. Taking the more macho, difficult routes brought me to a span of about three feet between two large rocks. It was either leap from one to the other or use the perfectly situated stump wedged between them.

As fate would have it, I chose the stump, which as it turned out was *not* perfectly wedged. It only looked perfectly wedged, made to look that way by demons assigned to harass macho husbands. When my weight descended on it, it began to rock violently back and forth. I seized the moment to do my rendition of the funky chicken. For those of you unfamiliar with this dance from the '70s, picture a chicken with its head recently removed.

As gravity was taking its final toll, I spun around, catching myself on the two boulders, one hand on each. Staring into this no longer peaceful stream that was now six inches from my nose, and listening to my shrieking wife, I was trying to decide how to continue to look macho while at the same time favoring my now sprained right shoulder. Somehow, I managed to push my muscular frame up and onto one of the rocks, looking young and fit.

I mumbled something about strength and agility while my wife mumbled something about acting my age and a spastic, decapitated chicken. While I did perform well under the circumstances, I must admit my shift from rock to rock was anything but divine.

In short, I realized that how we handle transitions and cross over obstacles is important.

Four Divine Shift Verses

There are four divine shift verses in Scripture that have always been meaningful to me. I call them bridge verses. Each verse states that we transition from a particular level to another. Let's glean from them.

God's Wisdom Brightens Our Way

Proverbs 4:18 tells us that we go *from brighter to brighter* paths:

> The path of the righteous is like the light of dawn, that shines brighter and brighter until the full day.

In Scripture, light often represents revelation and truth. One of the synonyms for revelation is enlightenment, which actually comes from the Greek word *phos*—light. Enlightenment literally means to let in light. God wants to shine His light of revelation on our paths so that we might enjoy more and more success in our representation of Him and in our personal endeavors.

As part of the changing process and the newness He brings, the Lord takes us from one level of revelatory brightness to another. This deepening of our understanding enables us to move more effectively from stage to stage. Yesterday's revelation isn't sufficient for today. New levels of fruitfulness require new levels of knowledge and insight. We must have fresh bread—transition bread.

Not only must we have an increasing enlightenment of God and His Word, but we also need His light to "direct our paths" (see Prov. 3:6, *KJV*) in practical ways, on a daily basis. We face countless decisions on our journey, many of which will determine whether or not we continue to move forward. If we do not hear the Holy Spirit's leading, then rather than moving toward the next phase God has for us, we can suffer setbacks. We can miss *kairos* opportunities if the light of God's revelation is not consistently shining on our path.

Joshua and the Israelites suffered two serious setbacks in their campaign to take Canaan, one at Ai and one with the Gibeonites (see Josh. 7 and 9). Both setbacks were due to their failure to get direction from God.

Often the insight—light—we receive in current situations is actually meant to help us in the future stages for which God is preparing us. David learned this on his path to the throne of Israel. His declaration before facing Goliath—which certainly marked a shift in his life from *chronos* to *kairos*—was that the God who delivered him from the lion and the bear would also deliver him from the giant (see 1 Sam. 17: 34-37).

Many times when we find ourselves isolated, seemingly in a mundane, hidden place—as when David tended sheep—God is training us for a stage of visible victory and leadership. Though no one saw David kill the lion and the bear, the entire army of Israel saw him kill Goliath. Because the future is unknown to us, we frequently find ourselves asking, What is the purpose of this trial or battle? Why am I facing this distraction? Why am I being allowed to face this obstacle? What is the purpose of this lesson?

The answers may not be known for years, but be assured that God isn't wasting this season. The light of revelation that comes to you during these *chronos* times will be needed when you move into your destiny. In His grace and wisdom, God moves us progressively, and sometimes slowly, toward fullness. At the right time, the shift will occur.

Learn the lessons well. Remember, life's experiences are connected.

Acting in Faith Builds More Faith

Romans 1:17 says we go *from faith to faith*:

> For in it *the* righteousness of God is revealed from faith to faith; as it is written, "BUT THE RIGHTEOUS *man* SHALL LIVE BY FAITH."

Have you discovered that every new thing God does requires a new level of faith? If we are progressing in God—moving forward as He trusts us with more—He will constantly stretch us, which is both challenging and encouraging. He's preparing us for greater responsibility; and the faith He requires from us today is not the same as what He required from us yesterday.

Many Christians are satisfied with the status quo and have come to a place of stagnation. Remaining stationary in God is not an option, however. He wants to bring us to a qualitatively new and greater position of faith, which is necessary for the new things He wants to do.

In my journey with the Lord over the years, His assignments have increased in scope and difficulty. I recall feeling a bit overwhelmed when helping *individuals* who were walking through very trying situations. I learned many valuable lessons during those times, however, and God began to increase my assignments to *groups* of people—families, staffs, Bible school classes, a church, etc.

God in His mercy and wisdom starts us with small assignments that do not require a level of faith beyond our training and understanding. But He does expect us to grow—to go from faith to faith.

But everything shifted in my life when God began focusing me on *nations*. I had to move to an entirely new level of faith. It is one thing to speak to a person or group of people; it is another thing entirely to speak to a nation. It is one thing to address a demon; it is another thing to confront a principality.

The United States is firmly embedded in my heart now. Though I often think, when God gives an assignment, *Who, me?* I also know He wouldn't have created the shift if He had not adequately prepared me.

God in His mercy and wisdom starts us with small assignments that do not require a level of faith beyond our training and understanding. But He does expect us to grow—to go from faith to faith. If we do not, He cannot create the shift.

Several years ago, I found myself with several leaders in the Body of Christ at a strategy meeting for the nation. During the meeting, the Holy Spirit spoke very clearly to my heart, saying, "Don't say anything; it is not your time." Though I felt insecure and embarrassed about not participating, I managed to sit quietly, saying nothing. It was a hard lesson, but very important.

Had I not heeded His instruction, only God knows the mistakes I could have made and the messes I might have created. I make enough of them as it is. But I'm secure in the fact that He doesn't require perfection, only obedience, and I know I can trust His timing.

A few years later, while ministering in a national conference, I heard that same voice speak very clearly to me, "Be bold, son, this is your hour." I spoke with great anointing and power—His, not mine—and moved into another level of ministry. It was a divine shift.

Grow in faith. His timing is perfect, and your time will come.

God's Glory Transforms Us

Second Corinthians 3:18 says we go *from glory to glory.*

But we all, with unveiled face beholding as in a mirror the glory of the Lord, are being transformed into the same image from glory to glory, just as from the Lord, the Spirit.

The Greek word used for "glory" is *doxa*, which has the connotation of recognition. Giving glory to God is literally recognizing Him for who He is and allowing Him to be recognized in and through us.

As we are transformed into His image, He is recognized in us more and more. Thus, our ability to represent Him is increased, and He will be revealed in and through us in greater measure. God desperately wants to be recognized in us!

This glorification is a wonderful circular process. The more we see His glory, recognizing Christ in our lives, the more He can then be recognized in us. The end result is that the world can see Christ to a much greater degree.

Many of us in the Body of Christ have recently gone through a *chronos* season where God has been working diligently in us to bring us to a place where the world will no longer look at us indifferently or with cynicism. They will instead recognize something about us that impresses them—not us, but Jesus. When the time is right, He will create the shift to *kairos* and then fullness. The result will be harvest and perhaps great revival.

Paul, who wrote the verse in 2 Corinthians 3:18—"transformed . . . from glory to glory"—understood the process well. After his dramatic conversion, he waited in a *chronos* season for many years while God was "glorifying" him—making him look like Christ. When the time was right, God caused a divine shift, recorded in Acts 13, and allowed Paul to reveal Christ to the world.

He wants to do the same with us. As we allow the Holy Spirit to transform us, we will look more like Christ and less like ourselves. At each new phase of glory, He can trust us with more authority, influence and power. And we, like Paul, are released to show the world a clearer picture of Christ.

Let it happen. Move from glory to glory.

Through Tears Comes Strength
Psalm 84:4-7 says we go *from strength to strength*:

> How blessed are those who dwell in Thy house! They are ever praising Thee. How blessed is the man whose strength is in Thee; in whose heart are the highways to Zion! Passing through the valley of Baca, they make it a spring. The early rain also covers it with blessings. They go from strength to strength, every one of them appears before God in Zion.

The word "Baca" means weeping; therefore, the "valley of Baca" means the valley of weeping. We frequently refer to the difficult times and situations in life as valleys. As we pass through these valleys, if we understand how to walk, work and cooperate with God, then springs can burst forth from these seemingly lifeless places. A valley of death or destruction is transformed into a place from which the river of life flows. A barren, dry place can be transformed into a place of springs.

Notice that the new place of strength is actually born at Baca—the place of weeping. The Hebrew word used for "strength" is the word *chayil* from the root word *chuwl*. *Chuwl* is the Old Testament word for travail or giving birth to something. When we walk in faith and persevere through the hard places, God can use these difficult times to birth (*chuwl*) new places of strength (*chayil*) in us. Yes, they may result from travail and times of struggle but, like the butterfly leaving the cocoon, when we pass through the valley of Baca (weeping) we can make it a spring. Our destiny is not the cocoon of Baca; it is the flight of freedom and victory. The dry, barren places in our lives can become places from which the river of life flows and new strength is born.

The Scriptures say, "If we suffer, we shall also reign with him" (2 Tim. 2:12, *KJV*).

God has been doing much transforming work in the Body of Christ, which has been very difficult for some. Unfortunately, many Christians have not realized that the times of travail are often the conduit to bring us to new levels. Instead of persevering through these seasons, many have despised the Bacas in their lives and allowed bitterness to come into their hearts. Rather than going from strength to strength, they unwittingly choose to remain in Baca. They don't move from a place of plowing and sowing to one of reaping and blessing. They miss the shifting of the times and seasons God wants to do in their lives.

This word for strength—*chayil*—is also a word for army and for wealth. We must realize that we can fight more effectively and prosper to a greater degree because of having gone through the valleys of Baca than we would have otherwise. It may seem difficult; we may not understand what is happening at the time and we may even think we're losing ground. But if we are faithful to keep pressing on and allow God to use those times to do what He wants to do in our lives, He will transform these places into boot camps and springs of blessings. Once we're on the other side, we realize that we're stronger and prospering more in the Lord now than we were before.

We can and must go from one position of victory to another. We must go from one phase of the army to another—from enlistment to boot camp to infantry men and women, becoming a stronger army. Some will go on to special forces because they have allowed the Lord to move them from one phase to another.

Allow God to do what is necessary to bring you into the new things He wants to do in your life. He desires to bring us from one new *kainos* stage to another, and another, and another. In fact, He wants to bring us forth into *kainos kairos*—a new strategic, opportune time. From there, if we walk with Him faithfully and diligently, He will move us to fullness.

RENEWING THE MIND

1. Do you always immediately recognize the full significance of the revelations God brings to your life through various situations? What is the connection between your awareness and the different seasons you experience throughout your life?
2. Does God care whether or not you are making a conscious effort to move forward in your spiritual life? Can you think of times that have required different levels of faith? How has this encouraged you?
3. Explain why glorification is a circular process. How can your moving from "glory to glory" affect those around you? How will it change you?
4. Do you have any choice in what is produced by the valleys in your life? What do you focus on when you are in the times of Baca? Can you think of some examples of fruit that have resulted from your valley experiences?
5. Define "obedience" and how it is related to perseverance.

Keys to Unlocking the Shift

In this chapter we will look at nine keys from the first chapter of Joshua that will help us successfully make the divine shift with God from *chronos* to *kairos* and on to fullness. The Israelites were about to go through one of the greatest shifts in history. If we can remember the strategies God gave them, during our own transition times, that knowledge will greatly assist us in our pursuit of fullness.

Key #1: We Must Accept Responsibility to Do Our Part

God will do what only He can do; we must also do what He expects and requires of us during the time of transition. Don't make the mistake of overemphasizing the sovereignty of God. In other words, it is dangerous to believe that God will make sure we get to fullness, no matter what we do. The generation of Israelites who perished in the wilderness is proof that fullness is not automatically guaranteed.

Chapter 1 of Joshua marks the transition of Israel moving into their *kairos* season. Ultimately, if they followed the Lord completely, they would move on into fullness. Joshua 1:2 states: "Moses My servant is dead; now therefore arise, cross this Jordan, you and all this people, to the land which I am giving to them, to the sons of Israel."

In saying this, God was doing more than just telling Joshua that Moses was dead. Yes, Moses had gone away by himself, and God took him on to heaven without anyone being around to witness it. But God was also announcing to Joshua, "It's *your* time now. You can no longer look to the man who mentored you and made the decisions for the nation. You have been trained and equipped; now you are the one, Joshua. It's your turn. Accept the responsibility! You must rise up to your place of leadership and lead this people."

The fact that we have responsibilities in this process is also implied by the use of the word "giving" in the above verse. It is translated from the Hebrew word *nathan*, which means more than to give (in the sense of bestowing something upon another). *Nathan* means to give in the sense of an assignment. God's *gifts* are also His *assignments*. He is going to gift us with the fruitful stage. He will bring us into fullness. Though His gifts are coming, they are also assignments. There will be a part for us to play.

When God "gave" the land to Abraham and his descendants, He was saying more than, "I am giving you the land." He was also saying, "I am 'assigning' this land to you." They would have to go in and possess it, fulfilling the assignment of the Lord, in order for God to do through them what He wanted to do.

The same will be true for us. We will have to be faithful to do our part in the transition time, fulfilling the assignments of the Lord. We must act responsibly, walking in truth and wisdom. If we do, we'll reach fullness.

CHAPTER FIVE

Key #2: We Will Have to Move in Great Faith During the Transition Times

This is especially true as we approach fullness. Sometimes more faith is required to move into this stage than was needed in the *chronos* season. In Joshua 1:2 God said to Joshua, "Cross *this* Jordan," (italics mine). He was making the important distinction that it was not the Jordan of several months earlier or of a few months later, but *this* one that was in flood stage (see Josh. 3:15). It was probably a mile wide and very deep and, as far as these Israelites were concerned, impassable. But God told Joshua that he was going to take these people—men, women, children, animals, possessions—across *this* Jordan. What an incredible faith it took to receive this word from the Lord!

We, too, will face impossible situations and insurmountable odds at times when we are moving in the *kairos* stage toward fullness. It will require much faith. We will have to believe that God is going to come through and do His part—the impossible—in order to get us to where we need to be.

Frankly, sometimes a lot of faith isn't needed in the waiting times. These seasons of simply maintaining do require patience but may not necessitate a great amount of faith. But when God says it's time to move forward, there will be steps of faith required on our part. We must be ready to move in faith.

Consider this story:

As the drought continued for what seemed an eternity, a small community of Midwest farmers were in a quandary as to what to do. The rain was important not only in order to keep the crops healthy, but to sustain the townspeople's very way of living. As the problem became more urgent, the local church felt it was time to get involved and planned a prayer meeting in order to ask for rain.

The pastor watched as his congregation filed in. He slowly circulated from group to group as he made his way to the front in order to officially begin the meeting. Everyone he encountered was visiting across the aisles, enjoying the chance to socialize with their close friends. As the pastor finally secured his place in front of his flock, his thoughts were on the importance of quieting the crowd and starting the meeting.

Just as he began asking for quiet, he noticed an 11-year-old girl sitting in the front row. She was angelically beaming with excitement; and lying next to her was her bright red umbrella, poised for use. The beauty and innocence of this sight touched the pastor's heart. He realized this young girl possessed faith that the other people in the room seemed to have forgotten. The rest of the people had just come to pray for rain . . . she had come to see God answer.[1]

Key #3: We Must Be Very Flexible

Joshua 1:11 states: "Pass through the midst of the camp and command the people, saying, 'Prepare provisions for yourselves, for *within three days* you are to cross this Jordan, to go in to possess the land which the LORD your God is giving you, to possess it'" (italics mine).

After the Israelites had waited 40 years in the wilderness for the promise of God to be fulfilled, you would think He could have given them more than three days notice to pack up all their possessions and prepare to move on. Anyone who has ever moved knows how difficult it is to pack and uproot. But God said, "In three days, you are to cross."

The shifts of God can come suddenly. He has reasons for doing this. Sometimes He just doesn't want us to have a lot of time to think about it, because we would probably mess things up somehow. He wants us to move quickly without the paralysis of analysis—an often overused but accurate statement.

Unexpected events will also require flexibility. I can assure you that when the transition begins, especially when we are walking through *kairos*—the strategic, opportune stage—there will be unexpected opportunities and challenges. God will do things in ways we really didn't anticipate. We have probably envisioned how things should happen. God will most likely do it differently, however, and we must be very flexible.

I recall, on one occasion, asking God to move by His Spirit and give us revival. I was surprised by the question that leaped in my spirit. I knew it was the Holy Spirit asking this: "What if I come riding on a donkey?" I realized immediately what He meant. He was referring to Christ coming to Jerusalem on a donkey (see Luke 19). He did not come the way they expected their King to come. He came lowly and humbly. In fact, no detail of His arrival transpired the way they thought it should. Sadly, they were not flexible enough in their theology and expectations to receive Him in this unforeseen turn of events. They rejected Him and, therefore, a mighty visitation (see Luke 19:44).

When He comes to us with divine shifts, requiring us to change and progress, He often does it in ways we do not expect. If He comes on a donkey, will we be flexible enough to flow with Him? One of the ironies of Christ's day was that the religious group that had kept alive the messianic hope—the Pharisees—was also the group that led the rejection of Christ. Why? Because

He did not come to them and act in the way they anticipated, and they were not flexible enough to accept it.

We mentioned earlier in this book the necessity of wineskins being new. One of the characteristics of a new wineskin is flexibility. Wineskins have to be flexible enough to expand with the pressure caused by the fermentation process. If unable to flex, the wineskin will burst, resulting in a destroyed wineskin and lost wine.

When God comes and begins to bring revival—when He moves in our lives—He will come in unexpected ways. There will be the pressures of expansion and change. The fermenting wine of the Spirit will expand us. If we cannot flex, we will lose the fruit in the *kairos* stage. Please stay flexible.

Key #4: We Must Remember the Basics

When Joshua was about to lead this generation of Israelites into their fullness, God put great emphasis on His Word. Joshua 1:7,8 states:

> Only be strong and very courageous; be careful to do according to all the law which Moses My servant commanded you; do not turn from it to the right or to the left, so that you may have success wherever you go. This book of the law shall not depart from your mouth, but you shall meditate on it day and night, so that you may be careful to do according to all that is written in it; for then you will make your way prosperous, and then you will have success.

God was bringing to Joshua's attention the vital importance of His Word. "Don't neglect the Word, Joshua. Keep it before you. Keep speaking it. Keep meditating on it. Then you will be successful."

When we are going through difficult times—and transition is certainly that—it is not the great, deep revelations of truth that keep us. It isn't our eschatology. It isn't our ability to exegete the Scriptures. It is the basics that keep us during times of transition.

Remember to focus on the Word. Remember to spend time with the Lord. Remember to fellowship regularly with other believers. Keep yourself in prayer. Do the basics!

During Christ's most vulnerable time—the temptation in the wilderness—He turned to the Scriptures. For us, too, as simple as it may seem, it is indeed the basics that keep us and ensure *success* during these times. You will prosper and have success if you do this.

On day six of the ill-fated mission of Apollo 13, the astronauts needed to make a critical course correction. If they failed, they might never return to Earth.

To conserve power, they shut down the onboard computer that steered the craft. Yet the astronauts needed to conduct a 39-second burn of the main engines. How to steer?

Astronaut Jim Lovell determined that if they could keep a fixed point in view through their tiny window, they could steer the craft manually. That focal point turned out to be their destination—Earth.

As shown in the 1995 hit movie *Apollo 13*, for 39 agonizing seconds Lovell focused on keeping the earth in view. By not losing sight of that reference point, the three astronauts avoided disaster.[2]

The basics are your reference points. Don't lose sight of them!

Key #5: We Need to Hold Fast to Past Promises

Joshua 1:6 states: "Be strong and courageous, for you shall give this people possession of the land which *I swore to their fathers to give them*" (italics mine). God called Joshua back to the promise He had made to Abraham and other forefathers. When we go through times of transition, it is imperative that we remember what God has spoken to us in the past. This will give us comfort, direction and something to which we can anchor.

Paul told Timothy to wage a good warfare through the prophecies that had been spoken over him (see 1 Tim. 1:18). In other words, during the difficult time Timothy was experiencing, Paul told him to go back and recall what had been spoken over him and to use those words as a weapon with which to fight. He was challenged to let the past affirmations sustain his faith.

This also served to bring Joshua an important perspective: What was about to happen wasn't only about them, but it was also about Abraham and others before them. And though not mentioned in this passage, it was about generations to come.

When God takes us to new levels or begins to shift us to levels of favor or success, we are often very short-sighted about it. We think it is simply to bless us or reward our faithfulness, when in reality it is often because of, and to bless, others. In Joshua's day God wasn't only rewarding this gener-

When God takes us to new levels or begins to shift us to levels of favor or success, it is often because of, and to bless, others and generations to come.

ation of Israel, He was furthering the redemptive purposes of history.

Remember that others will be impacted by your successful shifting.

Key #6: We Must Live in Complete Obedience

I realize this sounds so obvious that it seems I wouldn't need to mention it. After all, don't we always have to obey Him? Yes. But God greatly emphasizes obedience in this transition chapter. The word "command" is used eight times in the first chapter of Joshua. God commanded Joshua; Joshua commanded the leaders; the leaders commanded the people and God made reference to what He had previously commanded. The phrase "be careful to do" is used twice, as is the word "obey" or "obeyed." All together, the concept of obedience is seen 12 times in these verses.

During transition times, it is absolutely imperative that we obey the Lord and do it quickly. He knows how things must be done. We may not understand the importance of doing things His way, but He does, and it is essential that we do it His way.

Several years ago, I put together an "easy to assemble" swing set for my girls. While connecting these *2 million* "easy to assemble" pieces, I missed a step of the "easy to follow" instructions. Could this have been because the instructions were written by a nuclear engineer? I don't know. Nonetheless, I missed a step.

I finally reached a point, two weeks into the project, when step 50 couldn't be done because step 30 had been skipped. There was absolutely NO way to proceed without undoing steps 31 through 49. What did I do? Praised God for such a wonderful trial, of course, and spoke great "blessings" over the writer of those instructions. I then proceeded to undo and redo.

The Israelites were told to follow the Ark of the Covenant and watch it carefully because they had not passed that way before (see Josh. 3:4). We, also, are walking in ways and paths that are completely new. We need to follow the Lord carefully, waiting upon Him for direction, and obey Him, even when it may not seem the easiest or most exciting thing to do. God has a reason for doing it the way He does.

Key #7: We Need to Realize There Will Be Battles We Have to Fight

The fact that we've moved out of *chronos* into *kairos*, and perhaps even close to fullness—as with a mother who is delivering a baby—doesn't mean the struggle is finished. Victory may be very, very close, but often that is when the battle becomes the most intense.

God told Joshua: "Every place on which the sole of your foot treads, I have given it to you, just as I spoke to Moses" (Josh. 1:3). The word "tread" is translated from the Hebrew word *darak*. This word not only means to walk on, but it is even a stronger term that means a warrior's march or tread. A warfare term, it is the word used for "bending the bow" when about to shoot an arrow. This Hebrew word is still used today in Israel for the command, "Load your weapons." God wasn't telling Israel that everywhere they walked or stepped was theirs. He had already marked off the perimeters of the inheritance. He was saying symbolically, "Every place that you are willing to load your weapons and take, I'm going to give to you." God was telling Joshua that there would be a battle.

Destiny is always contested and we must know that the evil one will try to rob our destinies from us. He will try to steal from the Church the harvest that God wants to bring in this hour. He will try to keep us from experiencing the breakthroughs God wants us to have and for which we have been fighting or believing, in the areas of our family relationships, our health, our churches. The enemy will not give up easily. We are guaranteed success, however, if we fight the good fight of faith. But we will have to fight.

Key #8: We Must Recognize Our Need for Help

In verses 12-18 of Joshua 1, God mentions the tribes of Reuben, Gad and Manasseh, which had been given an inheritance on the east side of the Jordan. When given this inheritance, they had been told by Moses that they would still need to go and help their brothers take their inheritance. Joshua reminds them of that.

We are to see in this example the need to fight together—to stand together. It is important when we walk through difficult times and transitions to acknowledge our need for help. We need to humble ourselves and ask for prayer, counsel or encouragement. Don't hesitate to seek help; it is proper to do so.

For years, William Wilberforce pushed Britain's Parliament to abolish slavery. Discouraged, he was about to give up. His elderly friend, John Wesley, heard of it and from his deathbed called for pen and paper.

With trembling hand, Wesley wrote:

Unless God has raised you up for this very thing, you will be worn out by the opposition of men and devils. But if God be for you, who can be against you? Are all of them stronger than God? Oh, be not weary of well-doing! Go on, in the name of God and in the power of His might, till even American slavery shall vanish away before it.

Wesley died six days later. But Wilberforce fought for 45 more years and in 1833, three days before his own death, saw slavery abolished in Britain.

Even the greatest ones need encouragement.[3]

Wilberforce needed encouragement during a difficult time. Though the breakthrough happened many years later, perhaps this great milestone in history would not have occurred without his friend—Wesley's—encouragement.

Key #9: We Must Let His Peace Sustain Us

Joshua 1:9 states: "Have I not commanded you? Be strong and courageous! Do not tremble or be *dismayed*, for the LORD your God is with you wherever you go," (italics mine). The word "dismayed" comes from the Hebrew word *chathath,* which means to crack or break. Zodhiates uses the phrase "cracking under stress."[4] God was saying to Joshua, "This transition into your *kairos* stage and toward fullness will be stressful. There will be unexpected challenges, difficulties and warfare. While under the pressure of leading, Joshua, you are going to have to make sure you walk in peace. Don't crack under the stress."

Notice the word "let" in Colossians 3:15: "And let the peace of Christ rule in your hearts, to which indeed you were called in one body; and be thankful." We must *allow* the peace of God to rule. We have a choice. We can stress out by focusing on the problems and neglecting the basics, or we can take the time to quiet ourselves before the Lord and keep our faith strong. Consider this story:

A Queens, New York, woman leaned out of her eighth-floor tenement window and screamed for help. She was trapped in her bathroom. The inside knob had fallen off when her youngest child, age two, had closed the door from the other side. Two of her other children, ages four and five, were in the kitchen, alone, as supper cooked on the stove. The woman alternated between trying to break down the door herself and shouting to be heard. Both courses seemed futile and she was beginning to give up hope.

Meanwhile, a young man who lived twenty miles away happened to be visiting the neighborhood that day. From the street below, he heard the woman's pleas. He waved his hand to catch her attention and then screamed out, "I'm coming up to help you!" A short time later, she heard his voice from outside the bathroom door. "Listen closely," the young man instructed. "Put your fingers in the hole where the knob should be, pull it up, lift the door slightly and then quickly pull it open." The woman followed the stranger's instructions, and within moments the door was open.

Once freed from her temporary prison, she ran to check on the children. In response to their mother's screams, they had become upset and needed some coddling to soothe their cries. When all three children were safe within her view, the woman turned to the young man and asked in amazement, "How could you possibly have known how to get into my apartment, and how did you know how that door opens?"

"I know very well," he answered with a smile crossing his face. "I was born here. I lived in this apartment for fifteen years. I know how to get in the front door without a key. And the bathroom knob? It would always fall off, and we learned to open the door just the way I showed you!"[5]

As we move forward into God-given destinies, it is reassuring to know that God has already been there. Every *chronos*, *kairos* and fullness season He has seen before. The shifts—the "new" and "hidden" places—are only new and hidden to us.

God understands full well how to open the doors of breakthrough, victory and fruitfulness because He, the incarnated God, has been here before.

"I know your deeds. Behold, I have put before you an open door which no one can shut, because you have a little power, and have kept My word, and have not denied My name" (Rev. 3:8).

RENEWING THE MIND

1. What are your responsibilities before God to your family, friends, colleagues and country? How can you encourage those who have waited for months or years for something from God?

2. Which people, places and events serve to give your faith solace, strength and continuity? Why is it important to have such things during the various seasons of life?

3. What are specific steps you can begin taking right now to further your pursuit of God and His fullness?

4. Define God's peace in your life. Why is it important to have such peace as you transition through different stages in life?
5. Are you ready for the divine shift?

Bibliography

Gray, Alice. *Stories for the Heart*. Sisters, OR: Multnomah Publishers, Inc., 1996.

Halberstam, Yitta and Judith Leventhal. *Small Miracles*. Holbrook, MA: Adams Media Corporation, 1997.

Larson, Craig Brian. *Illustrations for Preaching and Teaching*. Grand Rapids, MI: Baker Book House, 1993.

Rowell, Edward K. *Fresh Illustrations for Preaching and Teaching*. Grand Rapids, MI: Baker Book House, 1997.

Steele, Jr., Richard A. and Evelyn Stoner. *Practical Bible Illustrations from Yesterday and Today*. Chattanooga, TN: AMG Publishers, 1996.

www.autoillustrator.com/online

Endnotes

Chapter One

1. Richard A. Steele, Jr., and Evelyn Stoner, *Practical Bible Illustrations from Yesterday and Today* (Chattanooga, TN: AMG Publishers, 1996), p. 180.
2. www.autoillustrator.com/online (accessed 10/16/00).
3. Alice Gray, *Stories for the Heart* (Sisters, OR: Multnomah Publishers, 1996), p. 268.
4. Edward K. Rowell, *Fresh Illustrations for Preaching and Teaching* (Grand Rapids, MI: Christianity Today, 1997), p. 43.
5. Craig Brian Larson, *Illustrations for Preaching and Teaching* (Grand Rapids, MI: Christianity Today, 1993), p. 193.

Chapter Two

1. Yitta Halberstam and Judith Leventhal, *Small Miracles* (Holbrook, MA: Adams Media Corporation, 1997), pp. 73, 74.
2. Edward K. Rowell, *Fresh Illustrations for Preaching and Teaching* (Grand Rapids, MI: Christianity Today, 1997), p. 118.
3. Ibid., p. 163.
4. Ibid.

Chapter Three

1. Richard A. Steele, Jr., and Evelyn Stoner, *Practical Bible Illustrations from Yesterday and Today* (Chattanooga, TN: AMG Publishers, 1996), p. 329.
2. Edward K. Rowell, *Fresh Illustrations for Preaching and Teaching* (Grand Rapids, MI: Christianity Today, 1997), p. 169.
3. Ibid., p. 100.

Chapter Five

1. Alice Gray, *Stories for the Heart* (Sisters, OR: Multnomah Publishers, 1996), p. 104.
2. Edward K. Rowell, *Fresh Illustrations for Preaching and Teaching* (Grand Rapids, MI: Christianity Today, 1997), p. 73.
3. Ibid., p. 46.
4. Spiros Zodhiates, *Hebrew-Greek Key Study Bible, New American Standard*, rev. ed. (Chattanooga, TN: AMG Publishers, 1990).
5. Yitta Halberstam and Judith Leventhal, *Small Miracles* (Holbrook, MA: Adams Media Corporation, 1997), pp. 122, 123.